Making Graphs

Pie Graphs

by Vijaya Khisty Bodach

Capstone press

Mankato, Minnesota

A+ Books are published by Capstone Press,
151 Good Counsel Drive, P.O. Box 669, Mankato, Minnesota 56002.
www.capstonepress.com

1 2 3 4 5 6 12 11 10 09 08 07

Library of Congress Cataloging-in-Publication Data
Bodach, Vijaya.
  Pie graphs / by Vijaya Khisty Bodach.
    p. cm.— (A+books making graphs)
  Includes bibliographical references and index.
  ISBN-13: 978-1-4296-0042-2 (hardcover)
  ISBN-10: 1-4296-0042-X (hardcover)
    1. Mathematics—Graphic methods—Juvenile literature. I. Title. II. Series.
  QA40.5.B6417 2008
  510—dc22   2007011075

Summary: Uses simple text and photographs to describe making and using pie graphs.

Credits

Heather Adamson, editor; Juliette Peters, designer; Wanda Winch, photo researcher;
    Kelly Garvin, photo stylist

Photo Credits

All photos Capstone Press/Karon Dubke except p.22 Dreamstime/Asiseeit
    and p. 24 Digital Vision.

Note to Parents, Teachers, and Librarians

Making Graphs uses color photographs and a nonfiction format to introduce readers to graphing
concepts. *Pie Graphs* is designed to be read aloud to a pre-reader, or to be read independently
by an early reader. Images and activities encourage mathematical thinking in early readers
and listeners. The book encourages further learning by including the following sections: Table
of Contents, Glossary, Read More, Internet Sites, and Index. Early readers may need assistance
using these features.

Table of Contents

Six friends gather around a whole strawberry pie.

The pie will be cut into six equal pieces.
Who wants some strawberry pie?

One friend in the group does not want
strawberry pie.

One slice is left in the pie tin.

A pie graph can also show how many
of these friends ate pie.
The circle stands for the whole group.

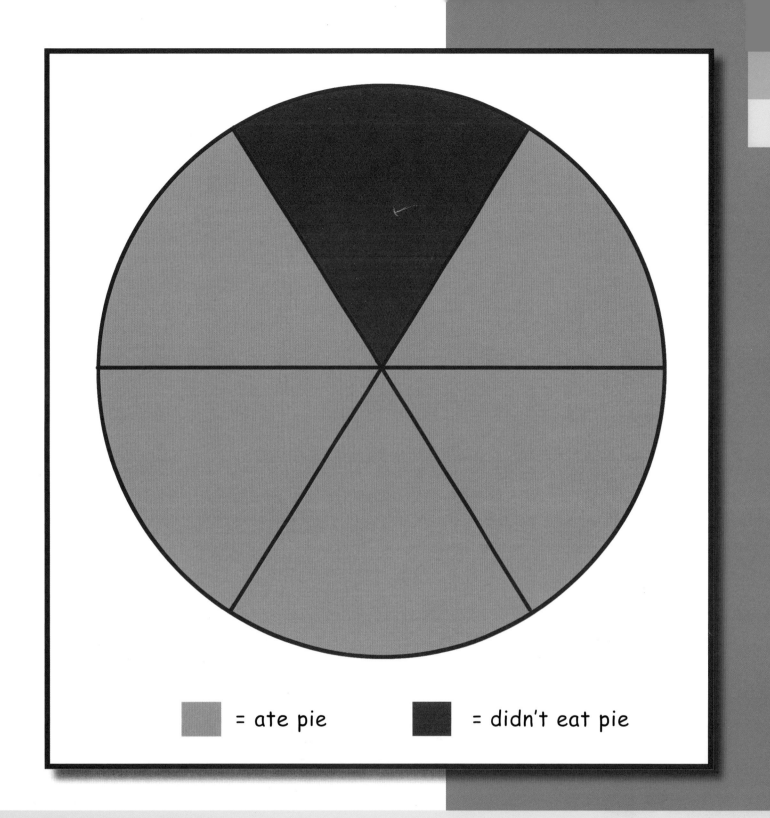

= ate pie   = didn't eat pie

The gray parts show how many kids ate pie.
The red part shows how many didn't eat pie.
It looks like the pie tin.

Pie graphs are not just for pies.
They show how parts compare to the whole.

The jump rope team has the same number of girls and boys. Two of each.

Jump Rope Team

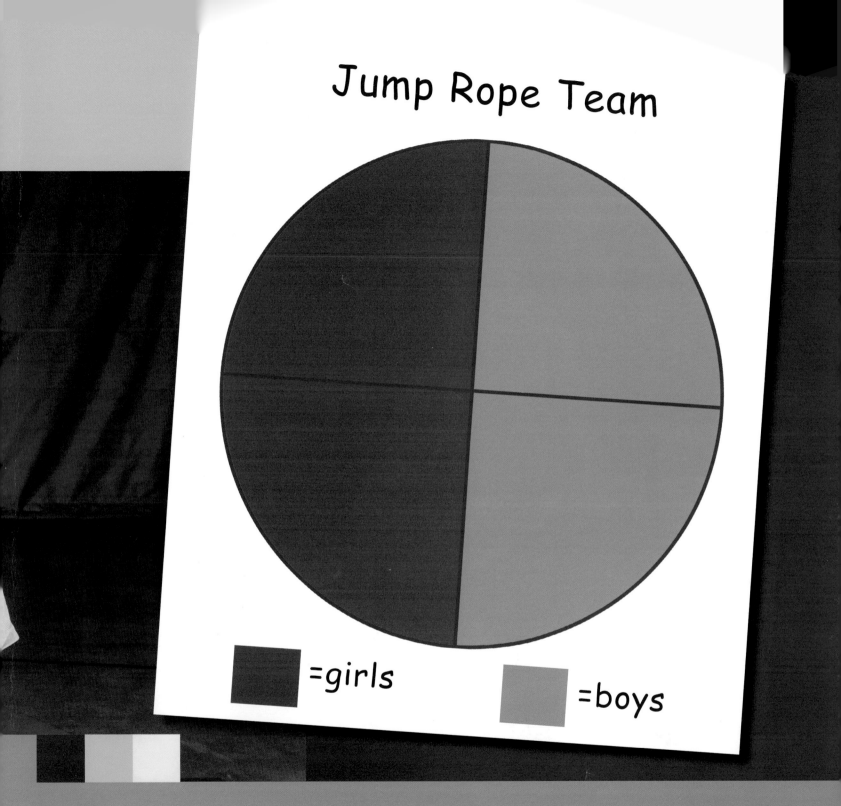

■ =girls   ■ =boys

A pie graph can compare the girls and boys.
The key shows pink for girls and blue for boys.
Half the circle is pink. Half the circle is blue.

Which kind of pizza is the favorite?
Let's make a graph of how much was eaten.

Favorite Pizza

cheese
pepperoni
vegetable

More people ate cheese pizza than
vegetable pizza. But pepperoni is
the most popular choice.

Which color apple do these children like the most?

Favorite
Color Apple

= yellow

= green

= red

Our graph shows most kids choose red apples.
Yellow apples are the least popular.

Yummy jelly beans! What flavor shows up most inside one package?

18

Use a pie graph to find out.
The whole package has ten beans.

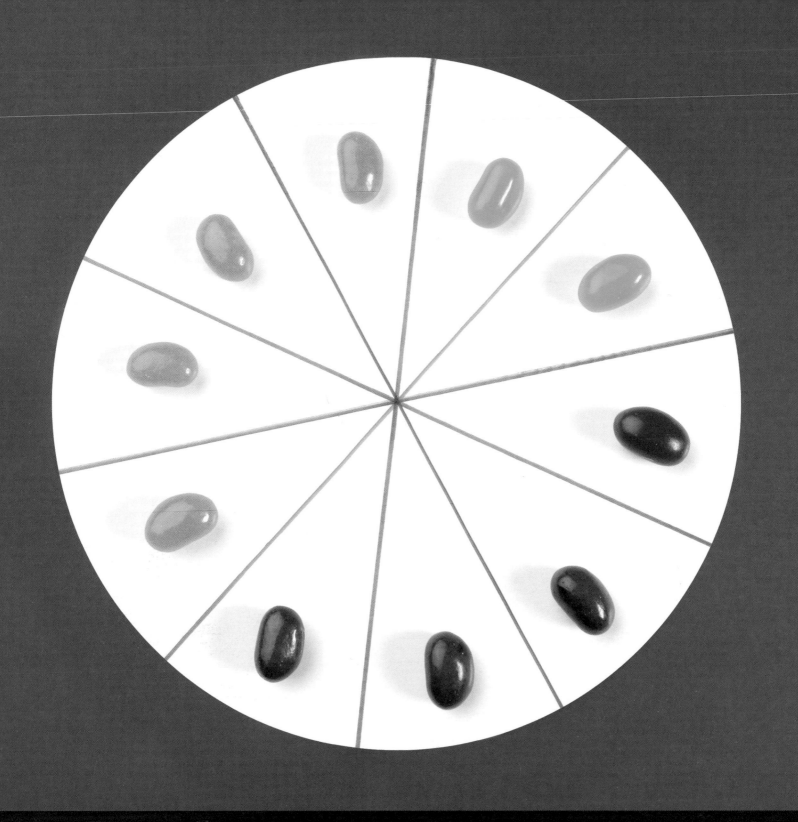

This whole circle has ten parts. Group the beans

Jelly Bean Flavors

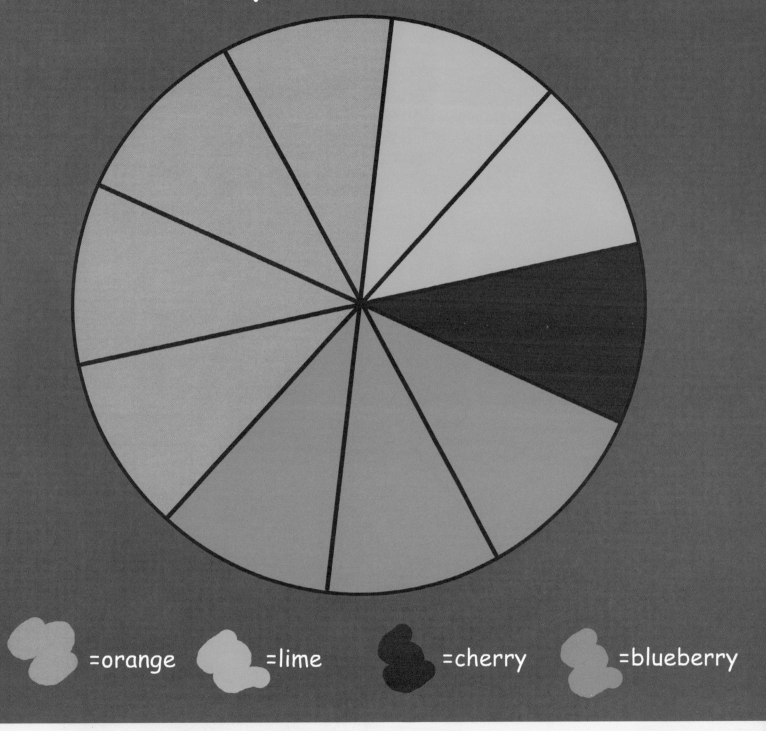

=orange   =lime   =cherry   =blueberry

Now make a graph to show the same thing.
The package has mostly orange beans.
It has few cherry or lime beans.

Sunday	Monday	Tuesday	Wednesday	Thursday	Friday	Saturday
	Math Quiz	Gym Class	Spelling Test	Gym Class	Show and Tell	

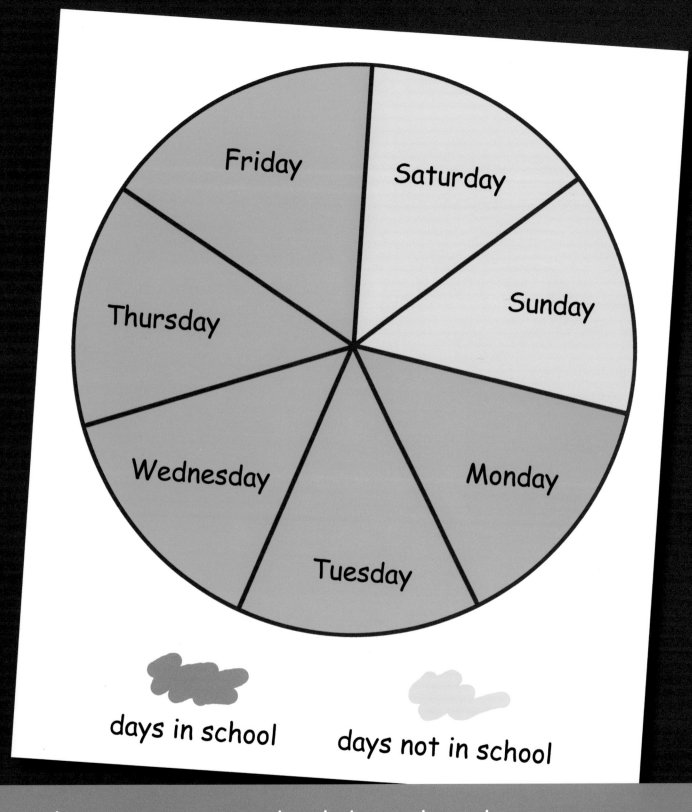

days in school

days not in school

There are more school days than days without school. The blue fills more of the circle than the green.

On a holiday week,
the graph looks different.

Sunday	Monday	Tuesday	Wednesday	Thursday	Friday	Saturday
	Math Quiz	Gym Class	Spelling Test	No School – Thanksgiving Break		

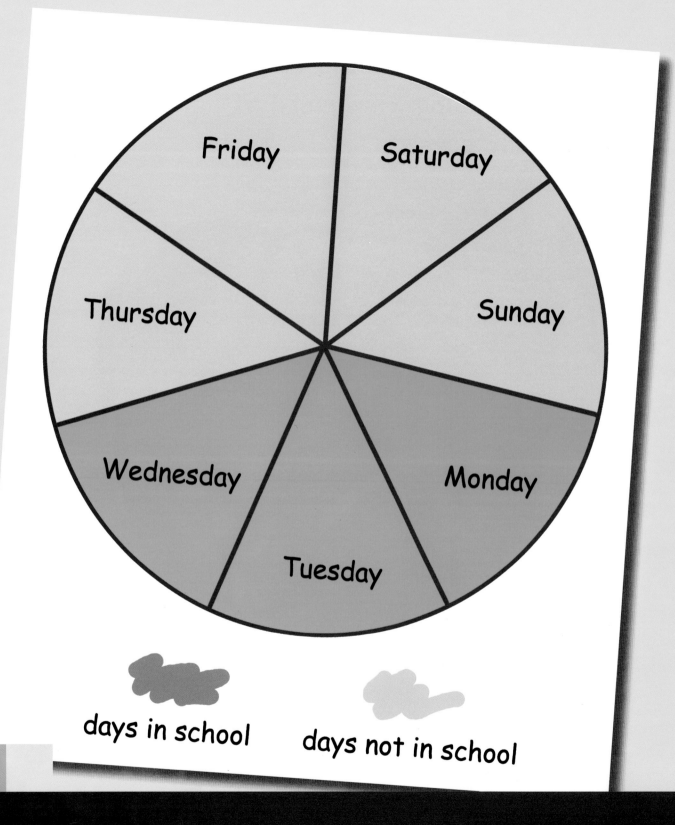

days in school

days not in school

The graph will show fewer school days
in a holiday week.

Jenna has four quarters. She puts one in her bank. She keeps out three quarters for spending. How much of her money did she save?

= money to spend

= money to save

The graph shows Jenna spends most of her money. She saves only a small amount.

There are 24 hours in a day.
How do you spend that time?
Make a pie graph of your activities.

How much of your day do you read,
eat, watch TV or play?

Do you think the pie graph would look
different on the weekend?

Glossary

compare (kuhm-PARE)—to judge one
thing against another

equal (EE-kwul)—the same as
something else in size, number,
or value

graph (GRAF)—a picture that
compares numbers or amounts;
graphs use bars, lines, or parts of
circles to compare.

popular (POP-yuh-lur)—most liked or
used most often

whole (HOLE)—all the parts of
something; the entire thing

Read More

Kernan, Elizabeth. *Let's Graph It!* Reading Room Collection. New York: Rosen, 2003.

Pistoia, Sara. *Graphs.* MathBooks. Chanhassen, Minn.: Child's World, 2006.

Internet Sites

FactHound offers a safe, fun way to find Internet sites related to this book. All of the sites on FactHound have been researched by our staff.

Here's how:

1. Visit *www.facthound.com*

2. Choose your grade level.

3. Type in this book ID **142960042X** for age-appropriate sites. You may also browse subjects by clicking on letters, or by clicking on pictures and words.

4. Click on the **Fetch It** button.

FactHound will fetch the best sites for you!

Index